DAY HIKES IN
LOS ANGELES

MALIBU TO HOLLYWOOD

by Robert Stone

Photographs by Robert Stone
Published by:
Day Hike Books, Inc.
114 South Hauser Box 865
Red Lodge, MT 59068
Layout & Design: Paula Doherty
Copyright 1997
Library of Congress Catalog Card Number: 96-96392

Distributed by:
ICS Books, Inc.
1370 E. 86th Place
Merrillville, IN 46410
1-800-541-7323
Fax 1-800-336-8334

TABLE OF CONTENTS

THE HIKES

MALIBU TO SANTA MONICA

HOLLYWOOD HILLS AND GRIFFITH PARK

About the Hikes

The Santa Monica Mountains are the only mountain range in California that runs east and west. Originally inhabited by the Chumash Indians, this twelve-mile wide mountain range divides the metropolis of Los Angeles in half, extending inland from the Pacific Ocean for fifty miles. With over 150,000 acres, the Santa Monica Mountains have lush verdant valleys, dense chaparral-covered hillsides, barren peaks, deep canyons, streams, abundant wildflowers in the spring, and a vast network of hiking trails.

The Day Hikes guide to Los Angeles focuses on scenic day hikes of various lengths. All of the hikes are in or near the Santa Monica Mountains, from Malibu to Hollywood. My goal is to share these hikes with you and others, enabling tourists as well as locals to enjoy the mountains with ease. People are often surprised to discover how many wonderful nature hikes are to be found just minutes from the urban sprawl.

All of these hikes require easy to moderate effort and are timed at a leisurely rate. If you wish to hike faster or go further, set your own pace accordingly. As I hike, I enjoy looking at clouds, rocks, wildflowers, streams, vistas, and any other subtle pleasures of nature. While this adds to the time, it also adds to the experience.

Although the hikes are accessible and enjoyable year around, they are more beautiful in late winter through spring when the creeks and streams are active and the foliage is lush green.

As for attire and equipment, tennis shoes, as opposed to hiking boots, are fine for any of these hikes. Sunscreen, drinking water, and a light hat are recommended. Pack a lunch for a picnic at scenic outlooks, streams, or wherever you find the best spot.

Enjoy your hike!

Malibu to Santa Monica

The Santa Monica Mountains contain several large state parks. Malibu Creek State Park spreads over 10,000 acres and contains over 30 miles of hiking trails. President Ronald Reagan's ranch is part of this state park.

Topanga State Park is a 9,000-acre undeveloped wilderness with 35 miles of trails that wind through canyons, over ridges, and past massive rock formations. Trippet Ranch, part of Topanga State Park, has a one-mile nature walk, a picnic area, and various trails leading into the backcountry. Among these trails is a portion of the Backbone Trail, which leads south to the Will Rogers Historic State Park. This 187-acre state park has a beautiful hike to Inspiration Point, a bare knoll overlooking Santa Monica Bay and West Los Angeles. On clear days, the Palos Verdes Peninsula and Catalina Island can be seen.

Within the Santa Monica Mountains are many beautiful canyons and streams to explore. Sullivan Canyon has a forest of sycamore, oak, walnut, and willow trees offering shade along its gently sloping trail, while Rustic Canyon has a year around creek flowing through steep canyon walls. Another year around stream is in the lush Santa Ynez Canyon. This trail also has a waterfall, fern-lined pools, and sandstone cliffs. En route to another waterfall, located in Temescal Canyon, is a footbridge, rock outcroppings, and caves.

To the south of the Santa Monica Mountains are the beach communities of Santa Monica and Venice. The famous Venice Canals, a pastoral residential retreat, is located inside the city near Venice Beach. Walking paths follow beside the canals, passing ducks and cottages, and cross the canals via arched bridges.

The major access roads to these hikes are the Pacific Coast Highway, Sunset Boulevard, Topanga Canyon Boulevard, Malibu Canyon Road, and Pacific Avenue. The hikes are on one of three United States Geological Survey topo maps—Topanga, Venice, or Beverly Hills.

Hollywood Hills and Griffith Park

Hollywood Hills and Griffith Park sit between the San Fernando Valley to the north, Hollywood to the south, Los Angeles to the east, and Beverly Hills to the west. The Golden State, Hollywood, and Ventura Freeways surround the hills and park on three sides. Each of these hikes is detailed on the Burbank and Hollywood United States Geological Survey topo maps and/or Hileman's Recreational and Geological Map of Griffith Park. The maps are available at the observatory. The elevations of these hikes range from 300 feet at the valley floor to 1,600 feet at Mount Hollywood.

Griffith Park, located at the east end of the Santa Monica Mountains, is the largest municipal park in the United States. It covers more than 4,100 acres. The park has a large variety of recreational facilities and tourist attractions, including the 75-acre Los Angeles Zoo, Gene Autry Western Heritage Museum, Griffith Park Observatory and Planetarium, Greek Theatre, Travel Town (a transportation museum displaying antique automobiles, planes, and trains), a bird sanctuary, an active 1926 merry-go-round, a horse riding stable, five golf courses, and over fifty miles of hiking trails that weave through the park's mountains and canyons. The trails have names and numbers, although signs are rare due to theft and vandalism. The trails are, however, well maintained, easy to follow, and safe to explore. The flat area of the park near its perimeter contains most of the tourist attractions. This leaves the mountainous interior and its steep canyons (more than 2/3 of the park) undeveloped, allowing for these hiking and horse riding trails. The chaparral-covered hillsides are filled with the sweet smell of sage and are home to deer, coyote, snakes, lizards, owls, and hawks. The canyons are dense with oak, sycamore, eucalyptus, and pine trees. While I have not covered all the hiking trails in this area, this cross-section of hikes offers an excellent sampling of the plant life, terrain, and views of the Hollywood Hills and Griffith Park.

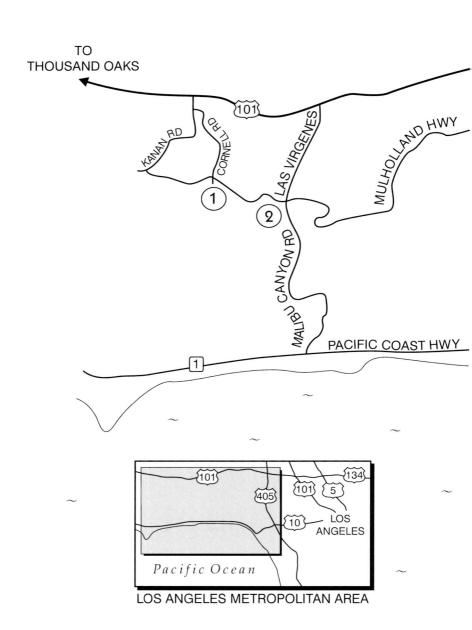

TO
THOUSAND OAKS

KANAN RD

CORNELL RD

101

LAS VIRGENES

MULHOLLAND HWY

1

2

MALIBU CANYON RD

PACIFIC COAST HWY

1

LOS ANGELES METROPOLITAN AREA

101

405

101

5

134

10

LOS
ANGELES

Pacific Ocean

MALIBU TO

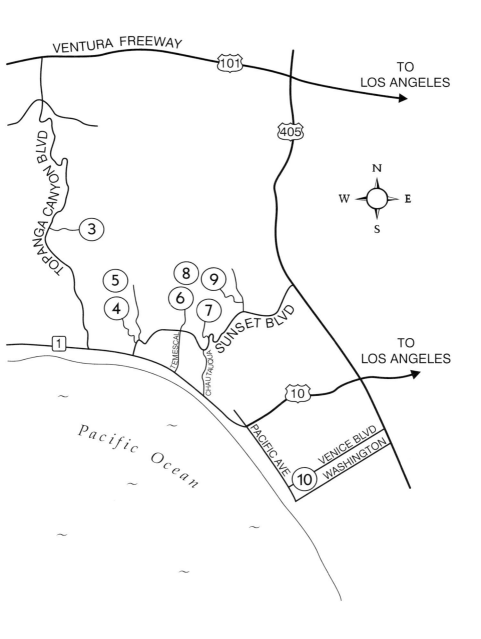

SANTA MONICA

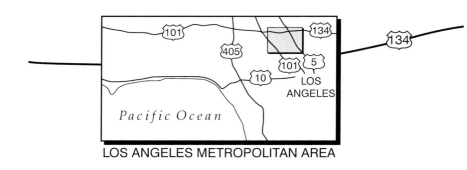

LOS ANGELES METROPOLITAN AREA

HOLLYWOOD HILLS

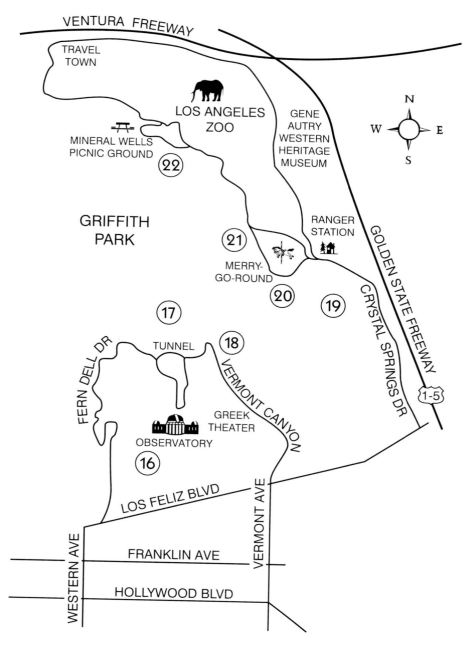

VENTURA FREEWAY

TRAVEL TOWN

LOS ANGELES ZOO

GENE AUTRY WESTERN HERITAGE MUSEUM

MINERAL WELLS PICNIC GROUND

(22)

GRIFFITH PARK

(21)

MERRY-GO-ROUND

RANGER STATION

(20)

(19)

GOLDEN STATE FREEWAY

CRYSTAL SPRINGS DR

I-5

N
W · E
S

(17)

TUNNEL

(18)

FERN DELL DR

VERMONT CANYON

GREEK THEATER

OBSERVATORY

(16)

LOS FELIZ BLVD

VERMONT AVE

WESTERN AVE

FRANKLIN AVE

HOLLYWOOD BLVD

AND GRIFFITH PARK

Hike 1
Malibu Creek State Park
Reagan Ranch Trail

Hiking distance: 3 miles round trip
Hiking time: 1.5 hours
Elevation gain: Level hiking
Topo: U.S.G.S. Malibu Beach
          Malibu Creek State Park Map

Summary of hike: This ranch was President Ronald Reagan's home in the 1950s and 1960s before he was elected governor of California. It now occupies the northwest corner of Malibu Creek State Park. The state park is host to a variety of outdoor activities including camping, fishing, horseback riding, and hiking. It is also home to many animals, including mountain lion, bobcat, coyote, deer, raccoon, snake, lizard, golden eagle, heron, and duck.
     The Reagan Ranch trails include a duck pond, a large rolling meadow, oak tree groves, stream crossings, magnificent views, and a visit to the Reagan barn.

Driving directions: From Santa Monica, drive north on the Pacific Coast Highway for 13 miles to Malibu Canyon Road. Turn right and continue 6.5 miles up this beautiful winding canyon road to Mulholland Highway. Turn left and drive 3.2 miles to Cornell Road. Turn left again and immediately park along Cornell Road wherever you find a spot.
     From the Ventura Freeway/101, exit at the Kanan Road offramp. Drive south 0.5 miles to Cornell Road. Turn left and continue 3.3 miles to the intersection of Mulholland Highway. Park along Cornell Road wherever you find a spot.

Hiking directions: From your parking spot, enter the ranch at a gateway through the white rail fence on the southeast corner of Mulholland Highway and Cornell Road. The unpaved road lined with eucalyptus trees leads toward the old Reagan

barn, 0.25 miles ahead. Continue past the barn to a footpath—
the Yearling Trail. The duck pond is on the left. Just beyond
the pond is the beginning of the loop portion of the hike. Stay
to the left on the Yearling Trail, heading towards the meadow.
As you hike through the meadow, there are two separate side
trails on the right that intersect with the Yearling Trail. You may
bear right on either trail. They connect with the Deer Leg Trail
for the return portion of the hike. To return, follow the Deer
Leg Trail as it winds past large oak trees and crosses Udell
Creek back to the trailhead.

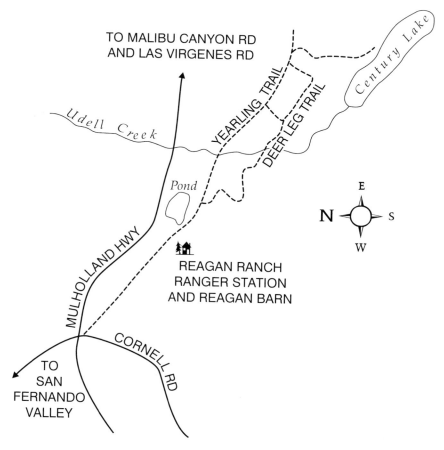

REAGAN RANCH

Hike 2
Malibu Creek State Park
Rock Pool and Century Lake

Hiking distance: 3 miles round trip
Hiking time: 2 hours
Elevation gain: 300 feet
Topo: U.S.G.S. Malibu Beach
           Malibu Creek State Park Map

Summary of hike: Malibu Creek State Park, purchased by the state from the 20th Century Fox movie studio in 1974, was originally home for thousands of years to the Chumash Indians. The park contains a Visitor Center, campground, a man-made lake, volcanic rock, sandstone outcroppings, majestic canyons, year around streams, and over 30 miles of hiking trails that spread over its 10,000 acres. This hike follows Malibu Creek to Rock Pool, surrounded by towering volcanic cliffs, and to the four-acre Century Lake. *Tarzan*, *Planet of the Apes*, and *South Pacific*, have been filmed here, to name a few, but it is most recognized for the *M*A*S*H* television series.

Driving directions: From Santa Monica, drive north on Pacific Coast Highway for 13 miles to Malibu Canyon Road. Turn right and continue 6 miles up this beautiful, winding canyon road. The state park entrance is located on the left, shortly before reaching the Mulholland Highway intersection. Turn left into Malibu Creek State Park. Park in the second parking lot on the left.

From the Ventura Freeway/101, exit at Las Virgenes Road. Head south towards the mountains for 3.5 miles. The state park entrance is located on the right, shortly past the Mulholland Highway intersection. Turn right into Malibu Creek State Park. Park in the second parking lot on the left.

Hiking directions: From the parking lot, cross the main road to the trailhead. Follow the High Road Trail as it slowly curves left alongside Malibu Creek to a bridge in the direction of the Visitor Center. Along the way, you will pass a concrete creek crossing on the left. At the Malibu Creek bridge, take the Gorge Trail to the right. (Crossing the bridge takes you to the Visitor Center.) Follow the trail a short distance, bearing left along the stream through a lava rock field to Rock Pool, 0.9 miles from the trailhead.

Return to the main trail back at the bridge. Take Crags Road, the main road, to the left. Continue on Crags Road uphill to a trail junction at the crest of the hill. From here you will be overlooking Century Lake and Las Virgenes Valley. The trail to the left leads down to the lake. Continuing on Crags Road leads to the M*A*S*H filming location. To return, retrace your steps.

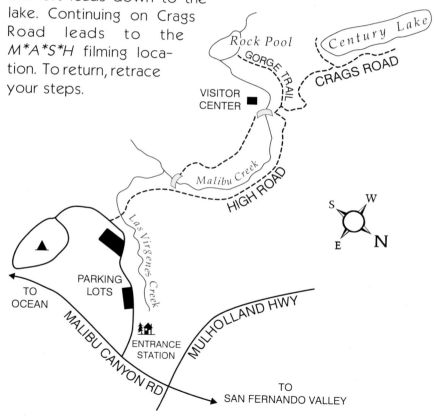

Hike 3
Topanga State Park – Trippet Ranch
Eagle Rock – Musch Ranch Loop

Hiking distance: 5 miles round trip
Hiking time: 2.5 hours
Elevation gain: 800 feet
Topo: U.S.G.S. Topanga
Trails of the Santa Monica Mountains

Summary of hike: This hike begins at a beautiful picnic area with a pond and a one-mile nature trail. The hike follows a fire road up to Eagle Rock, an impressive eroded sandstone rock covered with crevices and caves. The views of the mountains and valleys along this trail, including Santa Ynez Canyon, are superb. The return trail is a footpath that descends past oak, sycamore, and bay trees. The Musch Ranch Trail includes lush vegetation, ferns, moss-covered rocks, and stream crossings.

Driving directions: From Santa Monica, drive 4 miles north on the Pacific Coast Highway to Topanga Canyon Boulevard—turn right. Continue 4.6 miles to Entrada Road on the right—turn right. Drive 0.7 miles and turn left, following the posted state park signs. Turn left again in 0.3 miles into the Topanga State Park parking lot.

Hiking directions: The trailhead is located at the end of the parking lot by the picnic area. Follow the trail uphill a short distance to a posted junction. Take Eagle Springs Road—the left trail. 0.5 miles along this gradual uphill trail, you will pass the Santa Ynez Canyon Trail on t he right, which leads to a waterfall. Further along is the Musch Ranch Trail on the left. The trail forks in a short distance. Bear left to Eagle Rock ,which is very close and visually prominent.

From Eagle Rock, return to the Musch Ranch Trail junction. Take this footpath to the right as it winds down to the creek bottom through lush foliage and dense oak, sycamore, and laurel woodland. Two miles down this trail is a junction at the Musch Ranch Campground. Follow the trail sign and walk across the meadow. Turn left a short distance ahead at an unmarked junction and left again at a second unmarked junction. The trail winds back down to the Topanga parking lot, passing a pond along the way (photo on page 31).

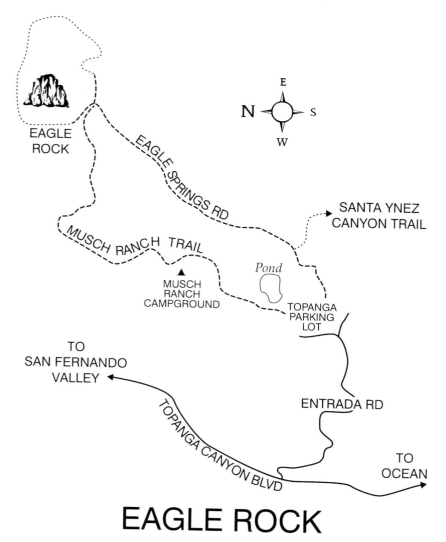

EAGLE ROCK

Hike 4
Topanga Overlook

Hiking distance: 5 miles round trip
Hiking time: 2.5 hours
Elevation gain: 1200 feet
Topo: U.S.G.S. Topanga

Summary of hike: This hike has vistas all along the trail, from Venice to Malibu and from West Lost Angeles to Topanga. The Topanga Overlook alone is worth the hike. It overlooks the Santa Monica Bay, Palos Verdes, and on clear days, Catalina Island.

Driving directions: Drive north on the Pacific Coast Highway, and turn right (inland) on Sunset Boulevard. At 0.3 miles, turn left on Paseo Miramar. Drive about one mile to the end of the road and park.

Hiking directions: Follow the fire road trail as it climbs up along the ridge. Just after two miles, take the trail to the left that leads to the Topanga Overlook. (Staying on the main trail will lead for another three miles to the Trippet Ranch, a park and picnic area in Topanga State Park.) The trail is easy to follow. Return the same way.

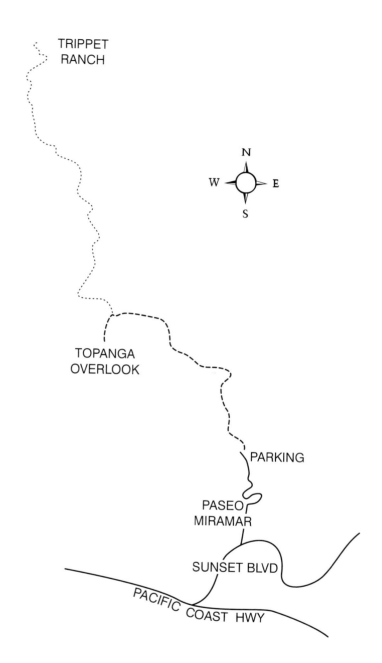

TRIPPET
RANCH

N
W ← ● → E
S

TOPANGA
OVERLOOK

PARKING

PASEO
MIRAMAR

SUNSET BLVD

PACIFIC COAST HWY

TOPANGA OVERLOOK

Hike 5
Santa Ynez Canyon Trail

Hiking distance: 3 miles round trip
Hiking time: 1.5 hours
Elevation gain: 300 feet
Topo: U.S.G.S. Topanga

Summary of hike: This trail is within the Topanga State Park. The sound of flowing water is constant during this hike. The hike includes many creek crossings using rocks as stepping stones. It is lush, forested, and cool. In the early morning, you will hear the music of croaking frogs. A 20-foot waterfall highlights this trail.

Driving directions: Drive north on the Pacific Coast Highway to Sunset Boulevard. Turn right (inland) on Sunset and drive to Palisades Drive. Turn left on Palisades Drive. Continue 2.4 miles to Vereda de la Montura. Turn left and park at the end of the road (approximately 700 feet).

Hiking directions: The trail begins at the creek and heads up the canyon. After about 10 to 12 minutes, there is a fork in the trail—stay left. Shortly thereafter is a second fork. This time, take the trail to the right. This trail will lead to the waterfall. The trail to the left leads deeper into the Santa Ynez Canyon. It ends 1.5 miles further at Trippet Ranch, a picnic and hiking area in Topanga State Park. Return by retracing your steps.

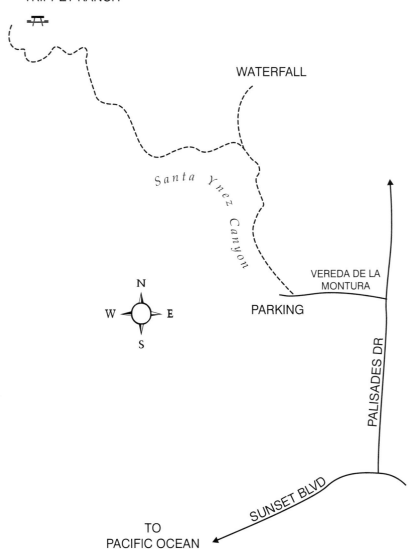

TRIPPET RANCH

WATERFALL

Santa Ynez Canyon

N
W ☉ E
S

VEREDA DE LA
MONTURA

PARKING

PALISADES DR

SUNSET BLVD

TO
PACIFIC OCEAN

SANTA YNEZ
CANYON TRAIL

Hike 6
Temescal Canyon

Hiking distance: 3 miles round trip
Hiking time: 1.5 hours
Elevation gain: 800 feet
Topo: U.S.G.S. Topanga

Summary of hike: This loop climbs up a ridge with scenic overviews of the entire Los Angeles Westside and the Pacific Ocean. The trail then descends into Temescal Canyon and returns along the canyon floor to the original parking area. Highlights include a footbridge overlooking a waterfall (photo on page 31), and Skull Rock, a sandstone outcropping that resembles a human skull (photo on page 27).

Driving directions: Drive north on the Pacific Coast Highway. Turn right (inland) at Temescal Canyon Road. Drive to the end of Temescal Canyon Road, north of Sunset Boulevard, and park at the entrance to the Presbyterian Conference Grounds.

Hiking directions: By the hiker registration booth at the far end of the parking lot, begin the hike to the left, climbing the west ridge of the canyon. Several switchbacks take you to the top of the ridge at Skull Rock. After viewing Skull Rock, return to the main trail for about a half mile. Watch for the trail on the left (east). This trail winds quickly down to the canyon floor, crossing a footbridge with views of the waterfall. The trail continues back to the parking lot, completing the loop.

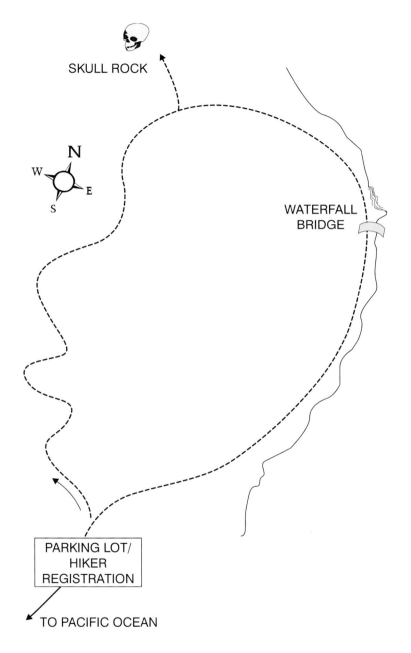

SKULL ROCK

N
W E
S

WATERFALL
BRIDGE

PARKING LOT/
HIKER
REGISTRATION

TO PACIFIC OCEAN

TEMESCAL CANYON

Hike 7
Will Rogers State Park

Hiking distance: 2 miles round trip
Hiking time: 1 hour
Elevation gain: 300 feet
Topo: U.S.G.S. Topanga

Summary of hike: This hike is a two-mile loop that starts and finishes at Will Rogers' home. The trail overlooks the Los Angeles Basin from downtown to the ocean. At the top of the loop is Inspiration Point, considered the best viewing area. Tours of Will Rogers' house may be taken daily. Picnic grounds with tables and horse riding stables help to make visiting this state park a wonderful way to spend the day.

Driving directions: Drive north on the Pacific Coast Highway to Chautauqua and turn right. Turn right again on Sunset Boulevard. Less than one mile from the corner of Chautauqua and Sunset, turn left at Will Rogers State Park. The parking area is at the end of this street.

Hiking directions: Take the well-maintained trail heading to the left from the Visitor Center, and follow it as it makes a two-mile loop. A hiking map is also available at the Visitor Center that shows other connecting side trails to the main loop. It is easy to read and follow.

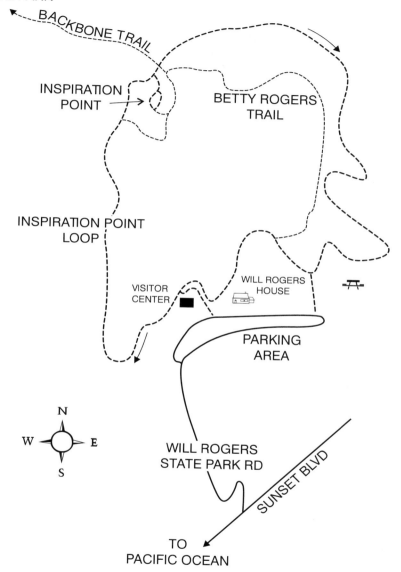

TO
TOPANGA
STATE PARK

BACKBONE TRAIL

INSPIRATION
POINT

BETTY ROGERS
TRAIL

INSPIRATION POINT
LOOP

VISITOR
CENTER

WILL ROGERS
HOUSE

PARKING
AREA

N
W   E
S

WILL ROGERS
STATE PARK RD

SUNSET BLVD

TO
PACIFIC OCEAN

WILL ROGERS STATE PARK

The Grand Canal in Venice - Hike 10

Path in Amir's Garden - Hike 22

The "HOLLYWOOD" sign – Hike 13

Skull Rock – Hike 6

Hike 8
Rustic Canyon

Hiking distance: 5 miles round trip
Hiking time: 3 hours
Elevation gain: 900 feet
Topo: U.S.G.S. Topanga

Summary of hike: This hike is more advanced. The first two miles are uphill. Along the ridge, Rustic Canyon is on the east while Rivas Canyon is on the west (back cover photo). The views are spectacular. At the base of Rustic Canyon, there is lush, overgrown vegetation and several old abandoned buildings.

Driving directions: Take the Pacific Coast Highway north to Chautauqua and turn right. Turn right again on Sunset Boulevard. Less than one mile from the corner of Chautauqua and Sunset, turn left at Will Rogers State Park. The parking area is at the end of this street.

Hiking directions: This hike is the beginning of the 55-mile Backbone Trail, which runs the length of the Santa Monica Mountains from Will Rogers State Park to Point Magu.
Beginning at Will Rogers State Park, take the main loop (Hike 7) for approximately one mile to the Backbone Trailhead. It is just past Inspiration Point and is well marked. Climb north along Chicken Ridge. After crossing a bridge at a saddle that separates Rivas Canyon and Rustic Canyon, watch for a trail on the right. This trail will quickly descend into Rustic Canyon. At the bottom of the canyon, follow the foot trail as it criss-crosses the stream. The canyon will narrow for one-third of a mile, then widen out again, leading back to Will Rogers State Park and the Visitor Center. Be careful of poison oak in the narrow canyon.

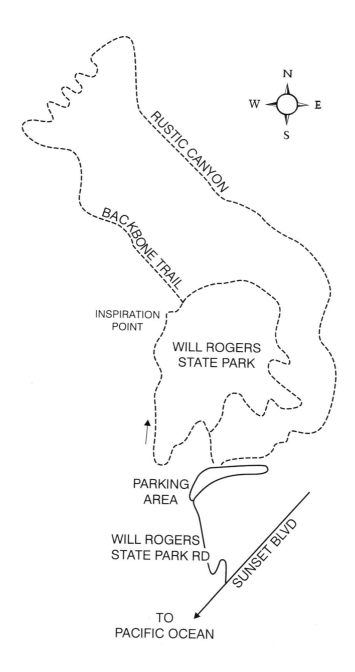

N
W — E
S

RUSTIC CANYON

BACKBONE TRAIL

INSPIRATION
POINT

WILL ROGERS
STATE PARK

PARKING
AREA

WILL ROGERS
STATE PARK RD

SUNSET BLVD

TO
PACIFIC OCEAN

RUSTIC CANYON

Trailhead to Mount Hollywood - Hike 17

Footbridge crossing stream - Hike 16

Waterfall in Temescal Canyon – Hike 6

Trail at Trippet Ranch – Hike 3

Hike 9
Sullivan Canyon

Hiking distance: 7 miles round trip
Hiking time: 3.5 hours
Elevation gain: 400 feet
Topo: U.S.G.S. Topanga and Beverly Hills

Summary of hike: Alive with the singing of birds, this hike sounds and feels like an aviary housed within huge stands of sycamore, oak, and willow trees. The near-level, open canyon is ideal for picnics.

Driving directions: Drive north on the Pacific Coast Highway to Chautauqua and turn right. Turn right again at Sunset Boulevard, and drive approximately 3 miles to Mandeville Canyon Road. Turn left on Mandeville Canyon Road, and turn left again at the first street—Westridge Road. Drive 1.2 miles on Westridge Road to Bayliss Road. Turn left on Bayliss Road and drive 0.3 miles to Queensferry Road. Turn left and park at the gate.

Hiking directions: Step around the ominous-looking gate that closes off the road to motor vehicles. Walk down the short service road to the beginning of Sullivan Canyon. Go to the right along the graveled trail of this canyon floor for 3.5 miles each way. This hike returns along the same trail, so you may hike a shorter or longer distance if desired.

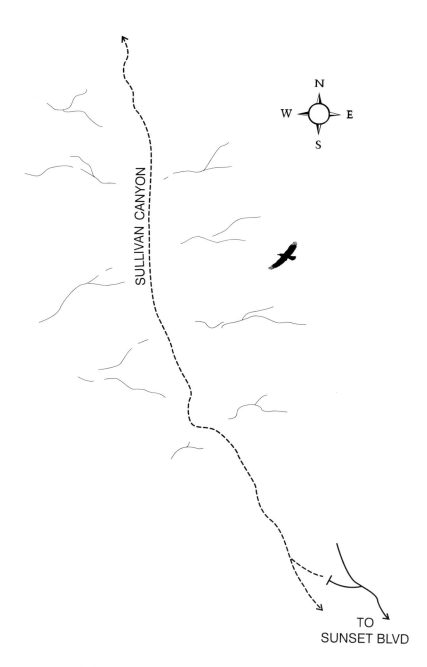

SULLIVAN CANYON

TO
SUNSET BLVD

SULLIVAN CANYON

Hike 10
The Venice Canals

Hiking distance: 1 mile or more
Hiking time: Variable
Elevation gain: Level

Summary of hike: Six interwoven water canals flow through this charming neighborhood (photo on page 26). Based on the canals of Venice, Italy, Abbott Kinney's "Venice of America" was completed in 1905. Landscaped walkways and diverse architecture make this hike an enchanting visual experience. Fourteen bridges and well-maintained walkways allow flexibility to walk around all six canals for any distance, direction, or length of time. Canoes, paddle boats, and ducks frequent these canals.

Driving directions: The Venice Canals are located near the Pacific Coast between Washington Avenue and Venice Boulevard, only two blocks east of Pacific Avenue, which parallels the ocean. Dell Avenue crosses over the canals via four arched bridges. You may park on Dell Avenue or anywhere along the residential street.

Hiking directions: Both sides of every canal have walking paths. You will be on the path from any direction entered.

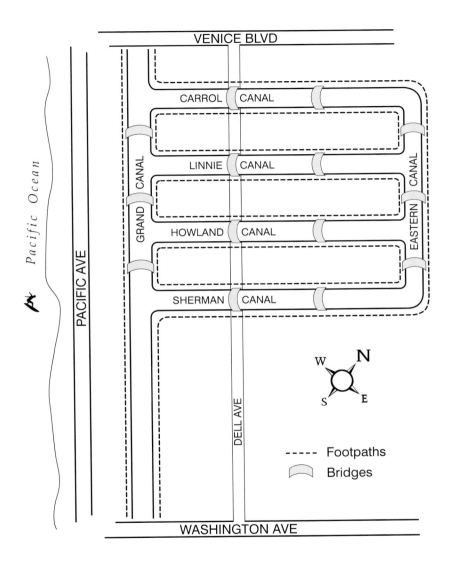

THE VENICE CANALS

Hike 11
Runyan Canyon Loop

Hiking distance: 2 mile loop
Hiking time: 1 hour
Elevation gain: 500 feet

Summary of hike: Runyan Canyon Park was purchased by the Santa Monica Mountains Conservancy and the City of Los Angeles in 1984. This trail loops around Runyan Canyon and crosses a broad gorge overlooking the canyon and the city. The trail passes the ruins of a pool house designed by Frank Lloyd Wright and lived in for several years by Errol Flynn. Remember, these are ruins, so use your imagination.

Driving directions: From Hollywood: At the intersection of Franklin Avenue and Highland Avenue, drive 0.3 miles west on Franklin to Fuller Avenue and turn right. Continue 0.5 miles to The Pines gate at the end of the road. Park along the street wherever a parking space is available.

Hiking directions: From the parking area, walk through The Pines gate into Runyan Canyon Park at the end of Fuller Avenue. A short distance past the entrance is a trail to the left. Take this trail as it curves to the right along the hillside parallel to the canyon floor. At one mile, the trail circles over to the east side of the canyon. Watch for a narrow trail to the right heading back towards the south. This trail leads to "Cloud's Rest," an exceptional overlook with a 360 degree panoramic view. The trail continues to the pool house ruins, then descends to the canyon floor and back to the trailhead.

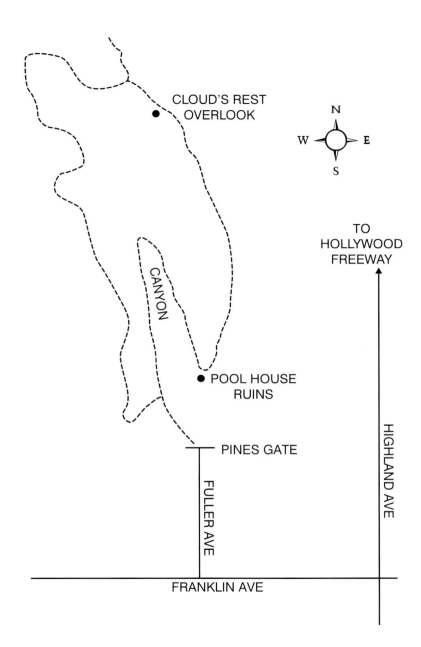

CLOUD'S REST
OVERLOOK

N
W · E
S

CANYON

TO
HOLLYWOOD
FREEWAY

POOL HOUSE
RUINS

PINES GATE

HIGHLAND AVE

FULLER AVE

FRANKLIN AVE

RUNYAN CANYON

Hike 12
Hollywood Reservoir

Open weekdays 6:30 - 10 am and 2 - 5 pm
Open weekends 6:30 am - 5 pm

Hiking distance: 4 mile loop
Hiking time: 1.5 hours
Elevation gain: Level hiking

Summary of hike: This hike follows the perimeter of the Hollywood Reservoir on an asphalt service road, closed to vehicles, with landscaping on each side. It is a rural retreat inside the city, frequently used as a walking and jogging trail. The tall foliage obscures full views of the reservoir except when you cross Mulholland Dam. The dam crossing is magnificent (cover photo). To the north is Mount Lee and the "Hollywood" sign overlooking the beautiful reservoir below. To the south is a view of Hollywood and the urban basin.

Driving directions: From Hollywood: Take Highland Avenue north past the Hollywood Bowl, curving left onto Cahuenga Boulevard. Continue one mile to Barham Boulevard. Turn right and cross over the Hollywood Freeway. Drive 0.2 miles to Lake Hollywood Drive and turn right.

From the Hollywood Freeway/101: Take the Barham Boulevard Exit, and head north 0.2 miles to Lake Hollywood Drive. Turn right.

Follow the winding Lake Hollywood Drive through a residential neighborhood for 0.8 miles to the Hollywood Reservoir entrance on the right.

Hiking directions: From the parking area, the reservoir entrance is on the right (south). The path follows around the perimeter of the reservoir, crossing the Mulholland Dam at the south end. The path then loops back to the road. It is a short walk along the road back to the parking area.

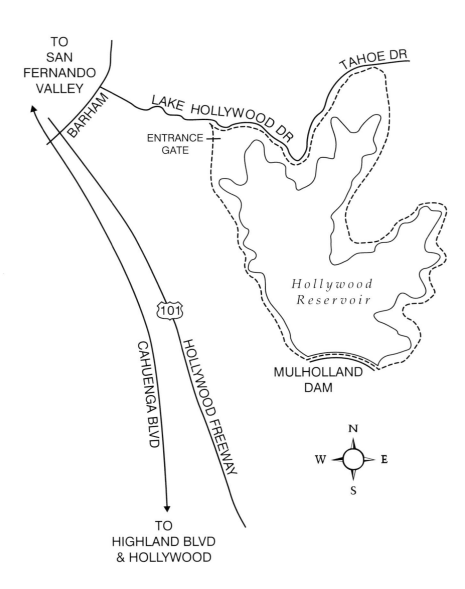

TO
SAN
FERNANDO
VALLEY

BARHAM

LAKE HOLLYWOOD DR

TAHOE DR

ENTRANCE
GATE

*Hollywood
Reservoir*

101

CAHUENGA BLVD

HOLLYWOOD FREEWAY

MULHOLLAND
DAM

TO
HIGHLAND BLVD
& HOLLYWOOD

N
W E
S

HOLLYWOOD RESERVOIR

Hike 13
Mount Lee
and the "Hollywood" Sign

Hiking distance: 3 miles round trip
Hiking time: 1.5 hours
Elevation gain: 550 feet

Summary of hike: This trail leads to the famous "HOLLYWOOD" sign on Mount Lee (photo on page 27). Originally built in the 1920s to read "HOLLYWOODLAND," promoting real estate development in Beachwood Canyon, the sign now measures 50 feet high by 450 feet long. In 1978, entertainment celebrities donated money to replace the original sign which was worn from time, weather, and vandalism. The sign sits just below the Mount Lee summit, and although the sign itself is fenced off from direct visitation, the views from atop Mount Lee are superb.

Driving directions: From Hollywood: At the intersection of Franklin Avenue and Western Avenue, drive 0.7 miles west on Franklin Avenue to Beachwood Drive and turn right (north). Continue 1.7 miles up Beachwood Drive to Hollyridge Drive. Park near this intersection.

Hiking directions: From the parking area, hike up Hollyridge Drive 200 feet to the trailhead on the left. From Hollyridge Trail, the "HOLLYWOOD" sign looms over the landscape. The Sunset Horse Ranch is to the left. Continue 0.5 miles to the unmarked Mulholland Trail. Take a sharp left up the trail as it heads west to Mount Lee Drive 0.3 miles ahead. At Mount Lee Drive, head to the right (uphill) to the ridge above and behind the sign. A hike to the left (downhill) leads to excellent frontal views of the sign. Return along the same path.

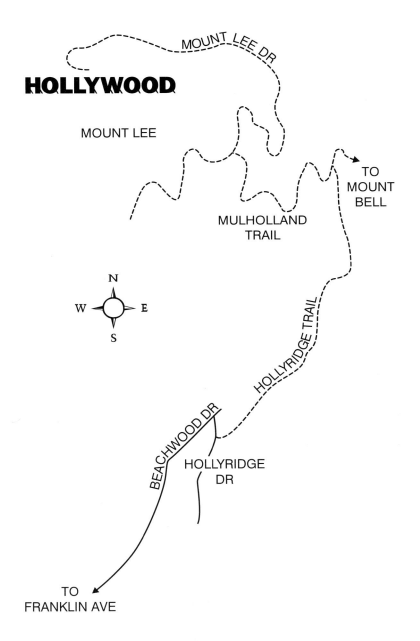

MOUNT LEE DR

HOLLYWOOD

MOUNT LEE

TO
MOUNT
BELL

MULHOLLAND
TRAIL

N
W E
S

HOLLYRIDGE TRAIL

BEACHWOOD DR

HOLLYRIDGE
DR

TO
FRANKLIN AVE

MOUNT LEE

Hike 14
Bronson Caves

Hiking distance: 0.6 miles round trip
Hiking time: 0.5 hours
Elevation gain: 40 feet

Summary of hike: This is a fun, short hike to Hollywood's most filmed caves. Originally a rock quarry, the crushed rock from the caves was used to pave the streets of a growing Hollywood. Many western and science fiction movie producers have shot on location at these man-made caves. *Star Trek*, *Gunsmoke*, and *Bonanza* have been filmed here, to name a few, but it is most recognized for the *Batman and Robin* series.

Driving directions: From Hollywood: At the intersection of Hollywood Boulevard and Western Avenue, drive 0.5 miles west on Hollywood Boulevard to Bronson Avenue. Turn right and continue 1.5 miles on Bronson Avenue, which merges with Canyon Drive, past Bronson Park to the end of the road.

Hiking directions: From the parking lot, hike back along the road 100 feet to the trailhead on the left (east) side of the road. The trail gently climbs 0.25 miles to the caves. From here you may walk through the caves and around the hill. Return along the same path.

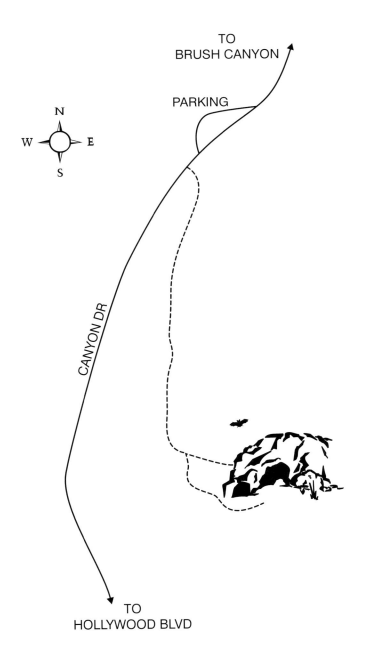

TO
BRUSH CANYON

PARKING

N
W E
S

CANYON DR

TO
HOLLYWOOD BLVD

BRONSON CAVES

Hike 15
Brush Canyon

Hiking distance: 2 miles round trip
Hiking time: 1 hour
Elevation gain: 500 feet

Summary of hike: Brush Canyon is a beautiful yet lightly traveled trail. Your hike begins within a forest of sycamore and oak trees. The trail climbs into a drier chaparral shrub terrain with views of the Hollywood area.

Driving directions: From Hollywood: At the intersection of Hollywood Boulevard and Western Avenue, drive 0.5 miles west on Hollywood Boulevard to Bronson Avenue. Turn right and continue 1.5 miles on Bronson Avenue, which merges with Canyon Drive, past Bronson Park to the end of the road.

Hiking directions: From the parking lot, hike uphill to the north past the vehicle gate. Continue on the fire road past the Pacific Electric quarry. At 0.25 miles is an expansive park and picnic area. After the park, the trail begins to climb, leaving the shade of the trees for the drought-resistant evergreen shrubs. Continue 0.75 miles to the Mullholland Trail junction. Take the trail to the right another quarter mile where the trail meets Mount Hollywood Drive. From Mount Hollywood Drive, return to your car via the same trail.

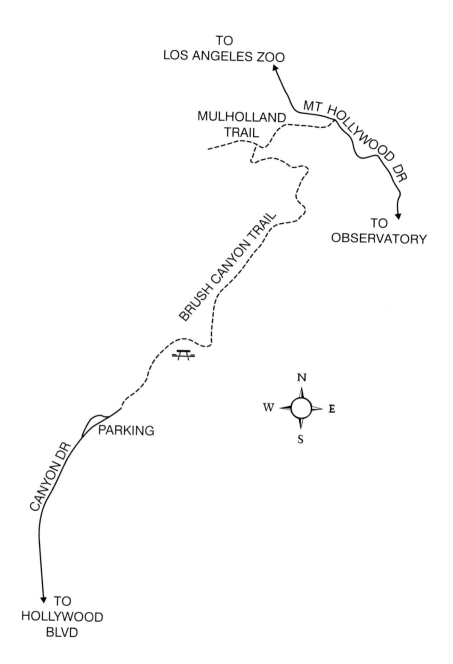

TO
LOS ANGELES ZOO

MULHOLLAND
TRAIL

MT HOLLYWOOD DR

TO
OBSERVATORY

BRUSH CANYON TRAIL

N
W E
S

PARKING

CANYON DR

TO
HOLLYWOOD
BLVD

BRUSH CANYON

Hike 16
Griffith Park Observatory
to Ferndell Park

Hiking distance: 2.5 miles round trip
Hiking time: 1.5 hours
Elevation gain: 500 feet

Summary of hike: This hike offers a panoramic view of the Los Angeles area, from the ocean to the San Gabriel Mountains. The garden pathways of Ferndell Park follow along a stream lined with moss-covered rocks. Charming footbridges cross the stream (photo on page 30).

The hike begins at the copper-domed Griffith Park Observatory (cover photo). The observatory has planetarium and laserium programs, a gift shop and various science displays. An observation deck with telescopes wind around the south side of this architectural landmark.

Driving directions: From Hollywood: On Los Feliz Boulevard, there are two ways to arrive at the trailhead parking lot. You may take Fern Dell Drive (north) 2.3 miles to the Griffith Park Observatory parking lot, or you may take Vermont Avenue (north) 1.8 miles to the observatory parking lot. Both directions offer a beautiful curving drive through the park.

Hiking directions: From the parking lot, walk towards the observatory. Take the trail to the left (east) of the observatory for 0.25 miles to a lookout point and trail junction. Take the right trail another 0.25 miles to the next junction. Go left along the Lower Trail (the shorter route) or right along the Upper Trail, and continue down to Ferndell Park. Stroll throughout the park along its stream, over the bridges, and through the beautiful fern-lined glen. To return, retrace your steps to the parking lot, taking either the Upper or Lower Trail on the way back.

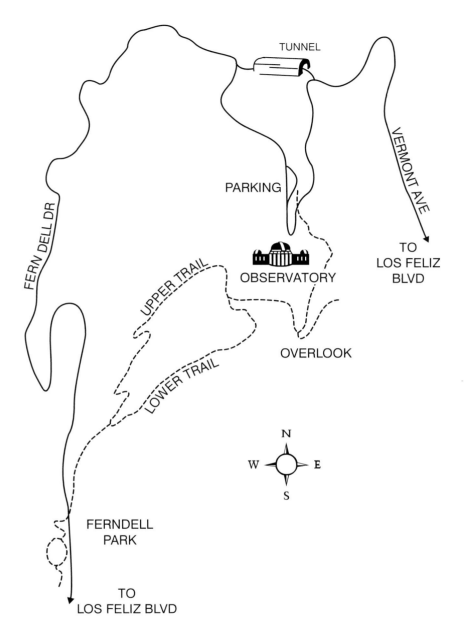

TUNNEL

FERN DELL DR

VERMONT AVE

PARKING

TO
LOS FELIZ
BLVD

UPPER TRAIL

OBSERVATORY

LOWER TRAIL

OVERLOOK

N
W E
S

FERNDELL
PARK

TO
LOS FELIZ BLVD

GRIFFITH PARK OBSERVATORY
TO FERNDELL PARK

Hike 17
Mount Hollywood Trail
and Dante's View

Hiking distance: 3 miles round trip
Hiking time: 1.5 hours
Elevation gain: 500 feet

Summary of hike: The Mount Hollywood Trail begins at the Griffith Park Observatory. The observatory, which opened in 1935, has excellent science exhibits and planetarium shows. Be sure to visit it before or after your hike.

The trail takes you to the top of Mount Hollywood and offers commanding views of the San Fernando Valley, the Los Angeles Basin, and San Gabriel Mountains. The trail also continues on to Dante's View, a terraced two-acre garden planted by Dante Orgolini in the 1960s. This south-facing garden has picnic benches and shade trees along its intertwining trail.

Driving directions: From Hollywood: On Los Feliz Boulevard, there are two ways to arrive at the trailhead parking lot. You may take Fern Dell Drive (north) 2.3 miles to the Griffith Park Observatory parking lot, or take Vermont Avenue 1.8 miles (north) to the observatory parking lot. Both directions offer a beautiful curving drive through the park.

Hiking directions: From the parking lot, hike north, in the opposite direction of the observatory, to the well-marked trailhead (photo on page 30). A short distance later, you will pass the Berlin Forest, a friendship park between the people of Berlin and Los Angeles. There are wonderful views and benches here where you can relax before continuing. At 0.75 miles, a junction indicates the beginning of the loop. The trail to the right is the shortest route to Dante's View and a joy to stroll along. Continue on the main trail as it curves around the hillside, opening up to views of the San Fernando Valley and surrounding mountains. A short trail to the left leads to a lookout at the top of Mount Hollywood. After enjoying the view, go back to the main trail and continue to the left, completing the loop and returning to the parking lot.

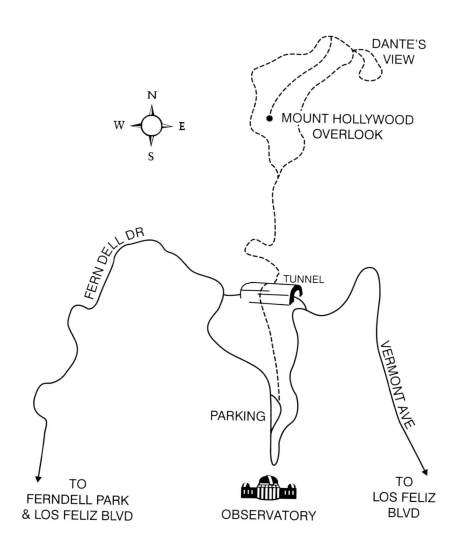

DANTE'S VIEW

MOUNT HOLLYWOOD OVERLOOK

N
W   E
S

FERN DELL DR

TUNNEL

VERMONT AVE

PARKING

TO
FERNDELL PARK
& LOS FELIZ BLVD

TO
LOS FELIZ
BLVD

OBSERVATORY

MOUNT HOLLYWOOD

Hike 18
Bird Sanctuary Loop

Hiking distance: 0.5 mile loop
Hiking time: 0.5 hours
Elevation gain: Level hiking

Summary of hike: This trail is shaded by large pine and eucalyptus trees with lush vegetation. Within this wooded glen is a footbridge crossing the pond and streambed. Beautiful rock walls line the pathways. It is very peaceful.

Driving directions: From Hollywood: At the intersection of Los Feliz Boulevard and Vermont Avenue, drive one mile north on Vermont, past the Greek Theater, to the Bird Sanctuary on the right side of the road. (The Griffith Park Observatory is 0.8 miles further.)

Hiking directions: From the parking area, walk to the right past the "Bird Sanctuary" sign. This well-defined trail leads through the sanctuary and back to the parking area.

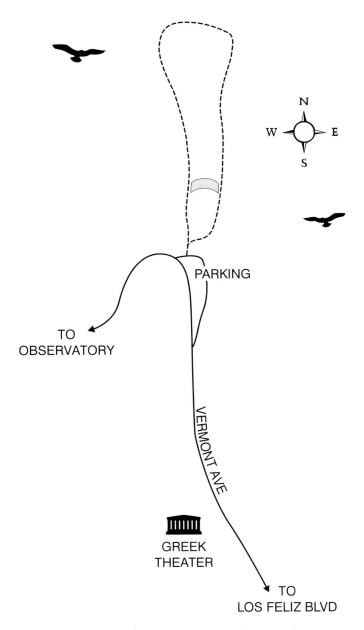

PARKING

TO
OBSERVATORY

VERMONT AVE

GREEK
THEATER

TO
LOS FELIZ BLVD

BIRD SANCTUARY

Hike 19
Beacon Hill

Hiking distance: 2.5 miles round trip or 4 mile loop
Hiking time: 1.5 hours or 2 hour loop
Elevation gain: 550 feet

Summary of hike: Beacon Hill is the easternmost hill of the 50-mile long Santa Monica Mountain Range. An illuminated beacon once resided on the top of Beacon Hill, warning aircraft of the mountains next to the Glendale Grand Central Airport, the main airport for Los Angeles and Hollywood during the 1910s and 1920s. From Beacon Hill you can see it all—from the ocean to the mountains and everything in-between.

Driving directions: From Hollywood: At the intersection of Los Feliz Boulevard and Crystal Springs Drive, located in the southeast area of Griffith Park, turn left (north) onto Crystal Springs Drive.

From the Golden State Freeway (I-5): Take the Los Feliz Boulevard Exit. Drive west a short distance to Crystal Springs Drive and turn right (north).

Continue 1.3 miles to the merry-go-round turnoff on the left. Turn left and park in the first parking lot.

Hiking directions: From the parking lot, walk back across the road and uphill to the right for 100 yards to a junction. Take the trail to the left heading uphill to the Fern Canyon Bridal Trail. Continue on the Fern Canyon Bridal Trail as it winds around the hillside. At one mile is a five-trail junction with benches. The trail to the left leads 0.25 miles to Beacon Hill. After taking in the views from Beacon Hill, return to the junction. If you wish to return along the same trail, retrace your steps to the right, back to the parking lot. If you wish to hike longer, take the left trail (Coolidge Trail), and continue one mile to a fork in the road. Take the left fork (Lower Beacon Trail), and return to the parking lot.

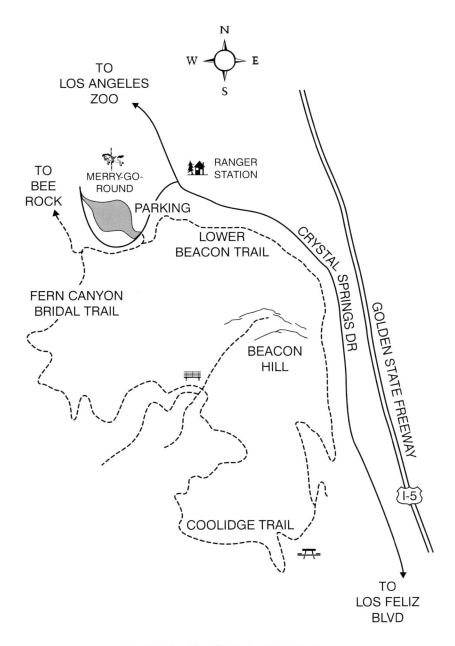

N
W E
S

TO
LOS ANGELES
ZOO

TO
BEE
ROCK

MERRY-GO-
ROUND

RANGER
STATION

PARKING

LOWER
BEACON TRAIL

FERN CANYON
BRIDAL TRAIL

BEACON
HILL

CRYSTAL SPRINGS DR

GOLDEN STATE FREEWAY

I-5

COOLIDGE TRAIL

TO
LOS FELIZ
BLVD

BEACON HILL

Hike 20
Fern Canyon Nature Trail

Hiking distance: 0.6 mile loop
Hiking time: 0.5 hours
Elevation gain: 150 feet

Summary of hike: This short nature walk takes you through a forested area along various trails, across footbridges, and to a natural amphitheater. It is located just minutes from the merry-go-round and the Old Zoo Park.

Driving directions: From Hollywood: At the intersection of Los Feliz Boulevard and Crystal Springs Drive, located in the southeast area of Griffith Park, turn left (north) onto Crystal Springs Drive.

From the Golden State Freeway (I-5): Take the Los Feliz Boulevard Exit. Drive west a short distance to Crystal Springs Drive and turn right (north).

Continue 1.3 miles to the merry-go-round turnoff on the left. Turn left and park in the first parking lot.

Hiking directions: From the parking lot, walk back across the road and uphill to the right for about 100 yards to a trail junction. Just before the junction is the Fern Canyon Nature Trail with a large sign inviting you in. All of the trails interconnect and loop back to the entrance. Choose your own path.

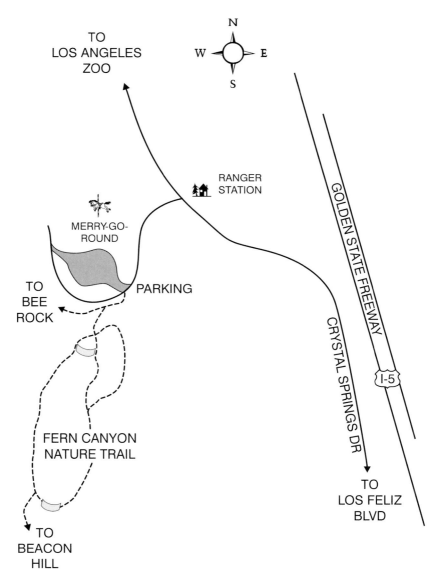

FERN CANYON
NATURE TRAIL

Hike 21
Old Zoo Trail
and Bee Rock

Hiking distance: 2.2 mile loop
Hiking time: 1.5 hours
Elevation gain: 300 feet

Summary of hike: This is a wonderful trail to a large sandstone outcropping in the shape of a beehive, called Bee Rock. There are great views of Griffith Park. The trail returns through the old Los Angeles Zoo along its walking paths, expansive lawns, and abandoned animal cages.

Driving directions: From Hollywood: At the intersection of Los Feliz Boulevard and Crystal Springs Drive, in the southeast area of Griffith Park, turn left (north) onto Crystal Springs Drive.
From the Golden State Freeway (I-5): Take the Los Feliz Boulevard Exit. Drive west a short distance to Crystal Springs. Drive and turn right (north).
Continue 1.3 miles to the merry-go-round turnoff on the left. Turn left and park in the first parking lot.

Hiking directions: From the parking lot, walk back across the road and uphill to the right for 100 yards to a trail junction. Take the Old Zoo Trail to the right, heading uphill into the trees. (The trail to the left goes to Beacon Hill, Hike 19.) At 0.5 miles, Bee Rock comes into view. Another 0.25 miles is the Bee Rock Trail junction to the left. On the right is the return route through the old zoo. Take the trail to Bee Rock. At 0.3 miles, the trail takes off to the left for the final ascent. This last section of the trail is steep, but the views make every step worth the effort.
After descending back to the junction, go through the gate and down along the paths of the old zoo, which has been converted into a park. All the paths lead back to the merry-go-round and the parking lot, completing the loop.

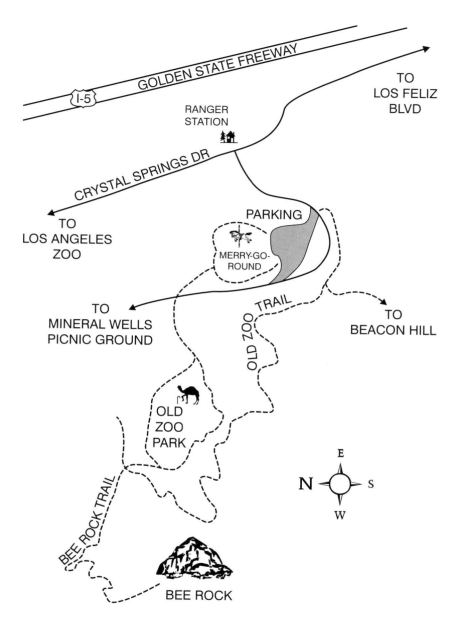

GOLDEN STATE FREEWAY

I-5

TO
LOS FELIZ
BLVD

RANGER
STATION

CRYSTAL SPRINGS DR

PARKING

TO
LOS ANGELES
ZOO

MERRY-GO-
ROUND

TO
MINERAL WELLS
PICNIC GROUND

OLD ZOO TRAIL

TO
BEACON HILL

OLD
ZOO
PARK

BEE ROCK TRAIL

E

N — S

W

BEE ROCK

OLD ZOO TRAIL
AND BEE ROCK

Hike 22
Amir's Garden

Hiking distance: 1 mile round trip
Hiking time: 1 hour
Elevation gain: 300 feet

Summary of hike: Amir's Garden is a beautifully landscaped, terraced hillside with rock-lined paths, benches, and picnic tables on the various levels of the hill. There is a wonderful network of trails and stairways leading through the garden (photo on page 26). Since 1971, Amir Dialameh has designed, planted, nurtured, and maintained this two-acre Eden.

Driving directions: From Hollywood: At the intersection of Los Feliz Boulevard and Crystal Springs Drive, in the southeast area of Griffith Park, turn left (north) onto Crystal Springs Drive.

From the Golden State Freeway (I-5): Take the Los Feliz Boulevard Exit. Drive west a short distance to Crystal Springs Drive and turn right (north).

Continue 1.5 miles to Griffith Park Drive (just past the merry-go-round) and turn left. Drive 1.3 miles to the Mineral Wells Picnic Area and park.

Hiking directions: From the parking area at the lower south end of Mineral Wells Picnic Area, take the trail to the right. A three-way junction is immediately in front of you. Take the middle trail up towards the water tank. 0.5 miles ahead is a lookout and a sharp trail switchback. Amir's Garden is at this lookout point. After strolling and enjoying the garden, return along the same path.

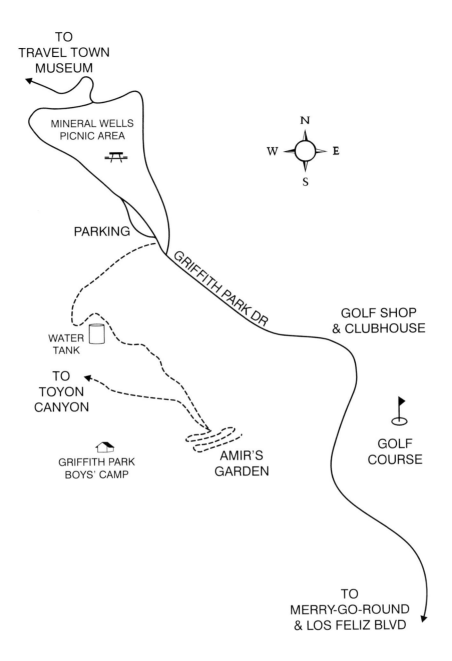

AMIR'S GARDEN

Bibliography

Appleberg, Marilyn J. *I Love Los Angeles Guide*.
New York: Collier Books, Macmillan Publishing, 1993.

Gagnon, Dennis. *Hike Los Angeles*. 3rd ed.
Santa Cruz, CA: Western Tanager Press, 1991.

Hileman's Recreational and Geological Map of Griffith Park.
3rd Ed. 1986.

McAuley, Milt. *Hiking Trails of the Santa Monica Mountains*.
5th ed. Canoga Park, CA: Canyon Publishing Co., 1991.

McKinney, John. *Day Hikers Guide to Southern California*.
Santa Barbara, CA: Olympus Press, 1992.

McKinney, John. *Walk Los Angeles: Adventures on the Urban Edge*.
Santa Barbara, CA: Olympus Press, 1992.

Riegert, Ray. *Hidden Coast of California*.
Berkeley, CA: Ulysses Press, 1989.

Schad, Jerry. *Afoot and Afield in Los Angeles*.
Berkeley, CA: Wilderness Press, 1991.

Stanton, Jeffrey. *Santa Monica Pier: A History from 1875 to 1990*.
Donahue Publishing, 1990.

Stanton, Jeffrey. *Venice, California: Coney Island of the Pacific*.
Donahue Publishing, 1993.

Trails of the Santa Monica Mountains (trail map).
California Coastal Trails Foundation, 1990.

United States Geological Survey 7.5 Minute Topographical
Quadrangles: Venice, CA, 1981; Beverly Hills, CA, 1981;
Topanga, CA, 1981; Burbank and Hollywood, CA;
Burbank, CA: State of California, 1972.
Hollywood, CA: State of California, 1981.

Wurman, Richard Saul. *L.A. Access*. 7th Ed.
New York: Access Press, 1994.

Information Sources

City of Los Angeles
Parks & Recreation
(213) 485-5555
(213) 485-5515
(213) 485-1310

Los Angeles County
Dept. of Parks & Recreation
(213) 738-2995
(213) 738-2961

Los Angeles Visitors Bureau
685 S. Figueroa St.
Los Angeles, CA
(213) 689-8822

Los Angeles Zoo (213) 666-4090
Merry-go-round (213) 665-3051
Observatory & Planetarium
(213) 664-1191
Western Heritage Museum
(213) 667-2000

Griffith Park
Visitors Center & Ranger Station
4730 Crystal Springs Dr.
Los Angeles, CA 90027
(213) 665-5188

Hollywood Chamber of Commerce
6290 Sunset Blvd. Suite 525
Hollywood, CA
(310) 469-8311

National Audubon Society
7377 Santa Monica Blvd.
Los Angeles, CA 90046
(213) 876-0202

Santa Monica
Chamber of Commerce
501 Colorado Ave.
Santa Monica, CA 90401
(310) 393-9825

Santa Monica Mountains
Conservancy
3700 Solstice Canyon Rd.
Malibu, CA 90265
(213) 456-5046

Santa Monica Mountains
National Recreation Area
30401 Agoura Rd. Suite 100
Agoura, CA 91301
(818) 597-9192

Santa Monica Mountains
District Headquarters
Calif. Dept. of Parks and Rec.
2860-A Camino Dos Rios
Newbury Park, CA 91320
(818) 706-1310

Sierra Club Foundation
2410 W. Beverly Blvd.
Los Angeles, CA 90057

Topanga State Park
Calif. Dept. of Parks & Rec.
20829 Entrada Rd.
Topanga, CA 90290
(310) 455-2465

Venice Chamber of Commerce
2904 Washington Blvd.
Suite 100
Venice, CA 90291
(310) 827-2366

Will Rogers State Historic Park
Calif. Dept. of Parks & Rec.
14253 Sunset Blvd.
Pacific Palisades, CA 90272
(213) 454-8212

Other Day Hike Guidebooks

___ Day Hikes on Oahu $6.95

___ Day Hikes on Maui 8.95

___ Day Hikes on Kauai 8.95

___ Day Trips on St. Martin 9.95

___ Day Hikes in Denver 6.95

___ Day Hikes in Boulder, Colorado 8.95

___ Day Hikes in Steamboat Springs, Colorado 8.95

___ Day Hikes in Summit County, Colorado 8.95

___ Day Hikes in Aspen, Colorado 7.95

___ Day Hikes in Yosemite National Park

     25 Favorite Hikes 8.95

___ Day Hikes in Yellowstone National Park

     25 Favorite Hikes 7.95

___ Day Hikes in the Grand Tetons and Jackson Hole, WY 7.95

___ Day Hikes in Los Angeles

     Malibu to Hollywood 8.95

___ Day Hikes in the Beartooth Mountains

     Red Lodge, Montana to Yellowstone National Park 8.95

These books may be purchased at your local bookstore or they will be glad to order them. For a full list of titles available directly from ICS Books, call toll-free 1-800-541-7323. Visa or Mastercard accepted.

- -

Please include $2.00 per order to cover postage and handling.

Please send the books marked above. I enclose $_____

Name _____

Address _____

City _____ State _____ Zip _____

Credit Card # _____ Exp. _____

Signature_____

1-800-541-7323

Distributed by:
ICS Books, Inc.
1370 E. 86th Place, Merrillville, In. 46410
1-800-541-7323 · Fax 1-800-336-8334

TOM EGENES

About the Author

This native Angelino has lived in the Rocky Mountains of Montana near Yellowstone National Park since the late 1970s. He still enjoys returning to Los Angeles to hike, explore, and enjoy good food.

Robert Stone has traveled, hiked, and photographed extensively throughout Asia, Europe, the Caribbean, Hawaiian Islands, and the Western United States.

This book is dedicated to my parents
for their love and acceptance in my various
adventures these many years.